My Gift to the Present

By: Dijon Noble

My work is consecrated to my forefathers and mothers, specifically to Tom and Wasutke Noble, and above all else to the "One Above".

ISBN 978-0-615-75444-4

Contents

If you were loaned something what would be your course of action in regard to what you were loaned? Wouldn't you use what was loaned to you to complete the purpose at hand, return it to its owner and go on about your business, would you take what was loaned to you and not care for it, not put it into use and disregard it? And if something is given to you in trust, of how much importance is it to you to display integrity and honesty, by taking care of and properly employing what was entrusted to you?

Taking all this into consideration does anyone consider the fact that this life on Earth is loaned to us? We all are given temporary custody and use of a body. All people have entered life on Earth through the birth canal of their mother and all people will exit and eventually disintegrate as an individual, and reintegrate into the environment from which they subsisted upon (accurately termed "Mother Earth"), so what is the purpose for which we were loaned this body?

If something in life is devoid of spirit it is without purpose, as our purpose in life is to manifest our spirit into physical reality, how is this known? Because if a people are subjugated and denied the physical resources along with the pleasures of life, they become a people in despair they lose their love of life and their purpose to live and thus their spirit becomes broken, their spirit is no longer present since the physical conduit for spirit is gone. All things necessary to life on Earth are found in abundance upon the Earth, all things on the Earth depend upon the Earth, which in turn depends upon the Sun, which depends upon the Universe as a whole, and as such the whole Universe is interdependent.

Thus through interdependence we are given the privilege of life and existence, it is lent to us and we are dependent upon the source of life that we cannot consider outside of ourselves (namely nature), because we are an extension of it, if we began to consider ourselves independent of natural things we would become unappreciative of our lives and what sustains us, we would exalt ourselves as self-sufficient and superior to nature, and separate from it, and thus lose our spirit and along with that our purpose of existence.

Does the present condition of life on Earth have no purpose? When the expression of nature reveals to us that all things are created free, all living beings were born to freely live and express their purpose, all food grows from bushes or trees, out of the ground, or develops from an embryo but all of it is free and grows freely, all shelter is obtained from the environment it consists of, it comes from wood or skins or perhaps from various kinds of stone but all of it comes from the Earth and it all comes freely, all water flows freely, so why are artificial conditions imposed on life?

Why do we have to pay for everything? Why must I acquire something I was born without when I was born with everything I require? How can we tell that we are living in unnatural conditions which isolate us from our purpose in life? Think about it, what does gold or silver matter to someone who has no food or water? To consider this deeper lets delve into the term "matter" you gain an insight into the minds of those who coined the term and you see that they are unconcerned and unfamiliar with spiritual things evidenced by the fact that what "matters" to them is matter.

II

So ask yourself is this life and the life you identify with only concerned with physical things, is that all that "matters" in life? Physical things which are subject to decay, whatever someone makes will decay and its level of importance will subside, unless it is of the necessities of life, food, water, shelter, etc. and you see that the things most important in life such as love, contentment, happiness, peace of mind, comfort, etc. are not physical things but they are made manifest in the physical, although they originate immaterially i.e. in the spirit.

It all originates in the spirit/immaterial realm even your physical "possessions", for instance, you had to have some initial desire to obtain those things. Your children were non-existent until you united with someone, and they became manifest through the intimacy of two people which is the physical union of emotions and desires creating a physical manifestation or body (the characteristics and traits of both parents into one body) it all originates with thought or emotion the physical channels of spirit.

Gold, Silver, Petroleum, Diamonds, Natural Gas, etc. are measurements of wealth in this man made condition imposed upon the Earth that we call the "world", but the wealth of the world is not necessary to life's continuance, these measurements of wealth originate in the Earth but are extracted in such a way as to harm it, destroying natural environments and the life that exists in these environments, they are removed simply for individuals to accumulate material possessions, but consider this a person in reality possesses nothing, we don't even possess our own body/life, so how can we claim to possess things outside of ourselves?

III

We cannot insure our health and extend our lifetimes, so how can we be the ones in possession of our lives, in truth the quality, wellbeing and length of our lives depends upon the Earth we live on and all the necessities it brings forth? Therefore the Earth in reality is the possessor of our lives, it has loaned us a body and what we need to sustain it, so we are indeed in debt to the Earth, and shouldn't wealth be those things that enhance our lives?

So how can people destroy the Earth which their lives depend on for temporal material possessions which do not enhance life? They can only be considered as devoid of spirit, that's why the only thing that matters to them is "matter", and within this artificial space people spend their lives, they spend their lifetime accumulating wealth and then spend the wealth, they "pay" attention to become educated in order to become employed, (which "employ" also means to use, so it implies that if you are unemployed you are useless).

They do all this in order to work and gain more currency until they are past their prime and no longer current i.e. retire and die in a state by which they tire of life, which is considered "A life well spent". The backward reality of this way of life becomes clearer when you realize that the exchange of this "wealth" comes from the circulation of paper composed of cotton & linen, both these ingredients come from plants, and in irony they say "money doesn't grow on tree's" but it certainly grows from plants which originate in the Earth, it has no innate value and is no different from anything else man-made that is impermanent on this Earth.

IV

All materials originated within the Earth, and through manipulation from its natural state becomes altered to the point where it's unrecognizable, cars, houses, clothing, furniture, money, whatever you see in the modern world can be broken down just as it was constructed, it can quickly go back to being an indistinct component of the Earth just as everything else will. Life in a natural condition cultivates and propagates what nature intended, growth, synthesis, interdependence, cohesion and continuance, it is apparent that unnatural conditions bring forth the opposite, so what fruit does the world and society at present bear?

It would be redundant to speak upon the present condition as it is obvious to all who live in it. In natural conditions everything is free and all things live in freedom, within an environment all life relies on each other, through the food chain & through the process of growth. In essence all life begins with the Sun, providing growth to plants which all living beings depend upon, plants move up the food chain being consumed by herbivores, which in turn provide sustenance to carnivorous and omnivorous animals which in turn provide life, shelter, clothing, and food to humans of that environment.

Humans in a natural environment almost always live communally and although it's not necessary to survive, communal living is therapeutic to the human spirit, so it was by nature the preferred method of life and it is preferred by all species, because even if a particular species lives alone for most of its life if it doesn't become communal at some point and commune with a mate it will not be able to replenish the species, so all species are communal in the course of creating communities.

V

So all nature is bound together and you find throughout nature interdependency, cohesion, synthesis, interconnectedness and the intimate need for all species to rely on one another, in other words love, isn't this love? Think about it, isn't this why people go through life? Most people's priorities consist of getting married and having children, accumulating wealth so they may attract or provide for a mate and offspring, as the adage goes "you can have everything in the world but if you have no one to share it with, it means nothing". In simplicity selfishness has no relevancy to life.

 If people are not communal as nature intended what is life to them? Living in lonesomeness until they die alone, formulating emotional bonds toward inanimate objects that cannot reciprocate emotion? Every human being has the common interest of wanting to fall in love, and let's consider that phrase "fall in love" when you fall don't you hurt yourself, don't you feel embarrassed and vulnerable and in pain, when you fall do you feel safe and secure and comfortable? And if you "fall in love" at what point do you get up and heal emotionally & physically? At what point do you recover from falling?

 Why do the people of the world want to fall in love rather than grow into love as nature intended? We don't fall in love with our brothers, sisters, mothers, fathers, etc. rather we grow into love with them, as we experience life with them we begin to relate to them hence the term relative, with a mate we begin to grow close to them through mutual experience, we relate to them and form a relationship, and become intimate and have relations in order to create relatives i.e. children & familial ties.

VI

I'm not saying you cannot experience love at first sight, when you see the Moon doesn't it conjure feelings of adoration and romance? When you see the Sunset does it bring forth awe and a sense of longing? And the same feeling is relevant between humans i.e. love at first sight, when you see someone and instantly relate to them. Yet in this present time it is hard to relate, ask yourself can you truly relate to yourself?

 Has your ideals, goals, thoughts and feelings regarding life been cultivated and brought forth by you? Did everything that makes you what you are come from within, or did it originate outside of yourself? Did it come from society in general, did the world mold your perception of life and existence or did you? And if the world molded your perception of life and existence you can never relate to yourself as the world is an artificial construct made up of concepts foreign to nature, so even when you obtain what the world tells you to, you still gain no fulfillment, as it is not sincerely what your heart wants, hence you cannot relate to others which brings us back to "falling in love".

 Falling is an act and that is what you see people do in place of relating, they "interact" and relationships become an activity, and you seek possessions so you can act the part that you feel the world wants you to portray, and in conclusion everything in life becomes an illusion, although you think you are close to what life is about, it becomes an illusion of closeness. So life is without purpose with nothing to relate to. We see nature naturally brings things that relate together, you see all species that are alike congregate and live together, as the saying goes "birds of a feather flock together" why do they flock together?

Living organisms flock together because they need one another to survive, to provide each other happiness, fulfillment and purpose in life and to continue their species, but if you live in an unnatural manner, for instance in the present time where society/ the world influences you to emulate everyone else and to express yourself exactly like the next person, you will never find someone with a nature like yours.

 Since you cannot draw them in with your nature, and most likely their nature is buried beneath formalities as well and by being influenced by the artificial & superficial society they become a character or an actor, whereas if they naturally expressed themselves like the saying goes "just be you" they would effortlessly attract people of like nature. A natural environment effortlessly attracts the species that belong there, they naturally form interconnectedness or what is termed an ecosystem, and even though you may think that since species eat one another, that this fact of life has nothing to do with love, in reality it does, as it is the highest form of love to sacrifice your life that another being may live, consider that.

 In a natural environment all food is alive and by the transfer of energy from one organism to another we see that life is death and death is life, as science has claimed to have discovered the fact that "energy cannot be destroyed but only transferred" the perfect example is that all earthly organisms transfer their life force to another in some way, shape, or form and ultimately back to the Earth as a whole, eating and the digestive process is the Earth passing through the Earth, returning to the soil in the same color variations, and contributing to its own fertility hence dung is also called "fertilizer".

VIII

Let's say I'm an artist and I paint many pictures, perhaps I lived centuries before my works became well known, those who see these paintings gain an insight into the nature of my life on this Earth, all of my feelings, ambitions, experiences, hopes etc. are condensed into these paintings, they are the embodiment of my earthly experiences according to my degree of expressiveness, and those who see them get an intimate understanding of me as an individual, perhaps even more so than those who knew me personally in my lifetime.

Taking into consideration this similitude it's easier to understand the "nature" of the architect/fashioner behind the works of nature, the immense and infinite design of the universe, the animals, the seasons, the stars, the landscapes and all living beings on Earth, so when I speak of the "One Above" I'm not speaking of above in time & space, but above comprehension.

At the time of this books publication it is estimated by various sources that there are roughly 7 billion people inhabiting the planet, there are between 100 billion and 300 billion stars in our galaxy (The Milky Way) and 100 billion galaxies in the visible universe alone. All these heavenly bodies are said to have come into existence around 13 billion years ago in what was termed "The Big Bang". Consider this; years are measured by the Earth's rotation around the Sun correct? this is the only measurement for a year from the perspective of humans so in reality there was no way of calculating this "Big Bang" since the Sun and Earth had not yet formed in order for the Earth to orbit the Sun and complete a 365 day cycle known as a "year".

Along with that what was in existence to perceive these years? Simply put if there is no one on the Earth to perceive a year then it doesn't occur since a year exists within human perception. What I'm trying to convey is the fact that human experience and perception has a limited scope and as such no one can ever wholly comprehend the works of nature and its creator/designer, despite the fact there is 7 billion people on Earth, 100–300 billion stars in our galaxy and 100 billion galaxies (which poignantly conveys human significance) mankind still attempts in vain to exalt themselves, and arrogantly proclaim they know the details of everything in existence, in spite of life's inherent mysterious nature.

 They even try to explain something so incomprehensible (the beginnings of the universe) with a simple theory, something that amounts to a guess, something that supposedly took place with no one and nothing there to corroborate, substantiate, and validate it. I'm conveying these truths, because it is the artist who alone can critique their work, pass judgment upon it, improve upon it etc. only the artist knows why they placed what where, why they gave certain characteristics to their creation, and if they haven't revealed when and where they made it no one would know, the details pertaining to their work are only known to them, it is a mystery to onlookers.

 So it is with the "art" of the one above comprehension, whose "artwork" or "works of nature" consists of all things within the natural realm of existence, and the universe and all it holds is indeed "A work of art" in the highest possible sense. Once again I'm not referring to "one above" as in time & space, as to be in time and space is to be physical.

X

In my work I'm referring to the creative energy that designs the physical reality, whose design permeates everything and is everywhere present since life is present in all things. I'm not referring to the God of Monotheism which exists within a body (Exodus 33:20-23) and was thereby designed, and is subject to the laws of physical reality and therefore is not above comprehension, I'm referring to the unseen designer behind life, which is also seen inherent in all life, and by this is in reality everything, but in the same way above everything.

 Illustrious examples of the work of this designer, so we may gain insight are animals. In the way they were made by nature they are exact and perfect in relation to the consciousness that created them, no animals are found to be outside of cohesion with their surroundings, they are specifically made to exist in a certain environment and their nature and qualities never deviate from that, by nature without which there would be no standard of perfect or imperfect they are perfect. According to the New American Webster Dictionary perfect is defined as. **per·fect**/ˈpərfikt/ *adj.* **1,** complete in every detail. **2,** without defect: flawless. **3,** of the highest type. **4,** exact: precise.

 They may not be perceived as that by the mind of mankind but they are perfect according to nature. Mankind cannot comprehend them, they cannot even make sense of their conflicting attitudes toward animals, as it is common for someone to say (in insult) "you are an animal" or "you are less than an animal" or for instance call someone a monkey or beast, but at the same time use them as the symbol of their country such as the American Bald Eagle, or name their sports teams after them or their automobiles.

XI

Why glorify the characteristics of animals by using these names to convey the majestic strength of a Lion or Bear, or the swiftness of a Falcon or Eagle or the endurance and speed of a Bronco or Ram, or the grace and agility of an Impala or Hawk? If animal character is looked down upon why would their names convey to you the highest sense of those characteristics they embody? If a human can be "less than an animal" then why are they admired so much that they are extracted from their natural environment and moved to an artificial habitat where they waste themselves away under captivity merely for the selfish amusement of onlookers?

 Consider for a minute the hypocrisy, how could someone in this society insult someone by calling them a monkey, yet monkeys saturate this society in movies, books and other forms of entertainment (Tarzan, Curious George, etc.), in them you highlight the lovable qualities of monkeys, their inquisitiveness, intelligence & charisma. The science of mankind (in the theory of evolution) accepts monkeys as their ancestors and according to this they came along many years before mankind, so I say to those who've evolved if you can't respect your elders at least respect your ancestors.

 How could society trick themselves into believing animals are inferior and worthless, when they use such phrases as "sly as a fox", or every dog has its day, or to compliment someone by saying they are as strong as an ox or they have a memory like an elephant, wise as a serpent or peaceful as a dove, or my favorite "free as a bird" mankind cannot denigrate the 2,000–3,000 mile migrations of the geese, the 10,000–12,000 mile grey whale migrations, or the 2,500–3,000 mile monarch butterfly migrations.
XII

Contemplate the intelligence of the spider, the dolphin or the crow. In nature, lion prides, prairie dog coteries, penguin colonies, baboon troops, flamingo flocks and countless other species on this Earth lead functional communal lives in working societies, what society amongst modern day man in the age of mankind (the world) is functional? Yet they still may insult someone by saying "You are less than an animal" or say "These people are animals" it would be a laughable joke if it wasn't a symptom of the worst form of delusion and hypocrisy.

It is complimentary for someone to call me an animal because life on Earth depends wholly upon animals, if there were no animals upon this Earth there would be no vegetation, without vegetation there would be no food and consequently no life at all. My ancestors and the ancestors of many other groups of people dispersed widely upon this Earth, who are the progeny of the Earth, lived with, depended upon, freely admired, named themselves after and clothed themselves with animals, and for that they were considered uncivilized and called animals, and in reality this is not so inaccurate because they and animals originated from the same source.

Ironically those who called them animals are just calling them "Living or Alive" if they understood the language they would know that animal comes from the Latin L. *animale* "living being, being which breathes," neut. of *animalis* "animate, living; of the air," from *anima* "breath, soul; a current of air." From which came the words animate, animation, animism etc. and by definition anything not animate or what is called inanimate is dead/lifeless, thus explains the jealousy and hatred in this world we see toward natural beings or more accurately the "Animosity".

XIII

An odd reality is that these same attitudes are directed toward nature as a whole, although man perceives the beauty of nature and perceives nature's characteristics in all things beautiful. Man may compare the beauty of nature with feminine beauty by say comparing the radiance and tenderness of a woman's smile with a flower, or her scent with a summer breeze or her bodily form with the graceful form of a rose, because the standard of beauty is in nature, it lies in the regal solidity of mountains, in the forlorn beat of the rain and the gentle rumbling of thunder, it lies in the rivers, springs, lakes and plains of the Earth, and the same essence that makes you see beauty in nature is the same essence that makes you see beauty in another person's form.

 It is the same that gives a lovable & adorable essence to a newborn child which makes other people want to nurture and take care of that child, so take into consideration the fact that the people you see beauty embodied in, that it is temporal, and also it is true that they didn't create themselves, so their beauty is not of themselves but of their creator, and that is exactly the same as the beauty of nature, all things change and all things natural tell of their maker.

 In light of this how can man say they are a part of the Earth, or that the Earth is their mother, yet they destroy it? When someone climbs a high mountain they say they conquered it, if someone clears an area of timber they say they tamed it, if someone mines something out of the Earth they say they exploited it (exploited the mineral resources), now would you conquer, tame or exploit your mother? Any civilized person wouldn't correct?

XIV

The term civil from which came civilized, has nothing to do with morals it means "pertaining to the state, its laws and administration" and only later came to have the connotation of courtesy or politeness, so those who had in their minds the notion of civilization & its propagation meant to spread law, what law? The individuals and environments that they brought civilization to were under the laws of nature with all things being in relation to each other and having freedom, so what civilization brought was the law of man and natures subjugation, and what does the law of man accomplish?

It breaks the cohesion, relations, and freedom and as such it breaks what you may call the web of life, so we see the laws of mankind made manifest, and with its appearance we see the destruction of the natural structure, a structure which life intended since life, nature and the universe are all unified, when you see nature you see a part of the universe and all life is contained within the universe and all life is nature and as such it is all under the same law, the law of its maker.

This law has been in place since immemorial thus it is the normal state of existence, the law of man is the abnormality and it is to be expected that in nature things return to normalcy, whenever there is an imbalance in the environment it becomes corrected and balance is restored, it is not normal that life becomes subjugated and humans become subjects of kings and queens, as I said they have no control over their own life so how can they consider themselves the ruling power over lives that they had no part in creating , it is not normal for humans to live as citizens (denizens of cities) and be civilians (persons under civil law).

XV

Before man existed and before the concept of time was implemented life was in existence and was regulated by the law of nature, before there were states with borders the state of life and existence was without borders, and now the state of life borders on destruction. Education or a career which are things that the world holds dear were nonexistent, as life itself teaches one what they need to know in order to survive and prosper within their particular environment, and you employ the skills you acquire in life in benefit of life's continuance.

 Through theft of life's resources mankind has become the law i.e. civilization, as such mankind has become the proverbial devil as well as the god, devil in regard to all the destruction and perversion (diversion of purpose) and god in the fact that in order to gain access to things of real value (food, shelter, water etc.) you must go to man in order to get a career or job in necessity, to acquire access to currency to gain the resources you need to continue your existence, when in reality man originated nothing of necessity to life whatsoever, as the only thing needed to sustain life is the Sun and the Earth.

 One constant in the universe/nature/life is that all things are alive and as such all things change, no living thing stays the same always and all things are living, even inanimate things originated within the realm of life, in the universe all things manifest, if not they are simply nonexistent and in life there is nothing nonexistent, everything has a present but not all things have a future or a past, but the laws of nature are ever present just as the universe as a whole and life is ever present, in the here & now. At one point in time the world didn't exist and as true as this is, at some point it will cease to exist, all things exist in the present and here is my gift to it.
XVI

My love is pure worship

Without beginning or end I wish I was familiar with what is contained within your perimeter, in awe I stand although emotions are elusive hence this feeling I cannot comprehend in a fleeting moment I failed to capture.

From my perspective I can only see the reflection of heaven so I reflect upon you always, hoping in my imagination that I will one day be embraced by your presence.

Since night and day only exists outside of your circumference, I wonder if you acknowledge my existence as I feel so insignificant, down here looking up.

When I gaze upon your essence I strain my neck and now that we see each other eye to eye complete darkness divided by blinding light, I realize only a minute portion of your appearance is contained within my sight.

And strangely I know your heart is the seat of my soul, and I will find rest there when I become fatigued with this life, although I became replenished when I realized what I longed for within the currents of time you alone can provide.

Therefore my love for you just like your gifts continually grow, and your acceptance is the highest relief as I know regardless of my actions I will still be admitted into your company.

You overlook my faults and strengthen my frailties and impart unto me life giving lessons, my love for you is my light so raise me like the Sun, forever set in the heavens.

You cannot take it with you

Why must I pay for everything yet I 'am told I 'am free they did their best to confine my heart and mind but my soul will forever roam freely.

Thus in the wind I will always find the provision of my needs, as the adversary of the Earth continually deceives regarding the nature of everything.

Ironically making its subjects believe paper doesn't proceed from the growth of trees, and if it is the root of all evil then from what soil did that root proceed?

And if evil causes its growth how has it grown to be your deity, the only wealth is the one of happiness, that's why I find you cannot purchase truth with fiction; indulgence leads to death if only the deaf would listen.

Would they follow a Savior and sacrifice their savings for salvation, I doubt for they take counsel from profit and meet prophets with derision.

They have turned the fertile Earth into a desolate prison, and what profit a man to gain everything in existence, when they have forfeited their privilege to live.

Gift to my Laureate

I would rather write freely than speak at a cost, by the generosity of your words I'm in debt to your heart, I wander without you so if I'm lost you can find me where you are, because surely I'm a priceless part of your heart and mind, and when you left I realized you meant the world to me, but my lust for the world turned your presence into a memory.

And by what standards am I bound to this world, I found by desire and also through lust, consider if I'm a ruler I'm bound to those I trust, considerate of truth as I write this, a ruler without trust becomes nothing more than a tyrant.

Thus I plead, forgive my tyranny, may your wise counsel polish my crown as I seek to find mercy in your eyes, and my jewel for you is my loyalty may it once again shine, my subjects please react softly to my mistakes I long for the populous to grow fond of me, because I exalted my kingdom on the throne of your mind but it is truly the heart where my authority lies.

Illusion of closeness

Although I recognize your face I do not know you.

I try to accentuate the truth in what I seen.

But to imagine a thing you desperately need but cannot reach,
only causes frustration compounded by grief.

My path would not allow deviate traits to infiltrate my mind state.

And by scarcity I have to assume I can obtain the will to abstain
from waste.

If you accompany me through this journey you will become
weary and fatigued which will only lead to your existence
becoming brief.

Because falsehood unknowingly enters righteous minds but dies
before it exits the teeth.

Farewell to the future

Is it real, when whatever in life that will occur with me fades into a vague memory, and when I'm gone my only gift would be my remembrance.

I became humble in mind when I realized I only exist in the present.

A race against time in hopes of advance, I look behind myself and find my opponent has already passed.

So with the fatigue of defeat I now see the past in front of me, frustration from consecutive losses gave way to the greater pain of exhaustion.

If time stretched forth its hands to me I would take my right of ownership, since I left behind what could have became mine when I held too close to the grip of caution.

Because I was slow to action and swift to imagine, running with loss of breath and tightened chest.

Yet what man in life, between the extremes of birth and death has ever seen every imagination of his heart made manifest?

Tempestuous Blessing

We intertwine like the branches of trees enjoined by the tones of a whispering breeze; we said nothing would come between us only to be separated by the swiftness of an unexpected tempest.

The seeds of potential blew away with the wind, I felt hurt when you turned away the embrace of my limbs, close in proximity yet never would we reach each other again.

I hope to sprout new growth and leave my hopes with past seasons, I can give so much shelter from rain, and comfort through shade but only if I'm needed.

I hope through the alternation of days past disappointments will fall from me, strengthening my roots and stimulating my patience.

But after incurring the hardship of bleak words and cold stares, I think the objective of my affection seeks to cut me down and lay my insides bare.

But I will receive this with pronounced resignation since my only wish is to be greeted with warmth as the days begin to lengthen.

Through many eyes

From within myself I shape my existence, the essence of life spread ornately it withstands the tempest.

I have raised up the living dead through the embrace of a translucent thread.

I will save my provision for lithe days as I lift my dwelling above the ground; it shines as it invites the company of the coming suns first rays.

The rain smiles upon me as drops accent what came forth internally, but which is outwardly heaven sent.

My eyes shine alike the moon light and have been held aloft in darkness.

I walk above the earth as my steps resonate in an octave, my arms and legs rotate as I weave the web of life by night and by day.

One without the other

If a butterfly flies past me I will not try to catch it,

Because I find that eyes tend to turn away from signs that show lessons,

And I don't know but its path of flight may be without direction.

I may find it to be no less than lost, and so I become grievous at heart to find the butterfly that I caught is no more than a moth.

And I cannot pursue when I'm immobile, because plenty were the days when ideals eluded those who were hopeful.

And one can no longer chase when the lust for love has escaped.

A most poignant grief in life is to see the natural ties of affection severed, but worst to see a lively flower growing alone in the desert.

No more than deserted and no less than neglected although imbued with life containing life giving nectar.

Thoughts of the transition

You slowly intrude upon my border lines until it becomes painfully obvious that you have invaded my mind.

The boundaries between us went within the span of a moment from an arm's length into a vast distance.

Yet an eternity is ample time as my thoughts are not bound by the confines of physics.

The ends of space are simply a step away and physical things are governed by the reality of my dreams as nothing is divided by senses.

I thought I began were the body ended but I see it will stop before I'm finished.

Hearts plea to mind

I approached and intended to know you I hoped to be closer to you than you are to yourself.

Without this I feel as if after having walked in perfect health I now lie down in the shadow of death.

In my path you are gone so now as I step I become forlorn.

But may you never have to mourn alone and be in confinement.

Didn't I release your fears to peace after confusion grew to violence?

Your thoughts clothed in darkness and my words held in silence.

You would be near me had you realized sustenance comes from what I announce.

I secured you in my sight and brought forth light from my mouth.

I called out to you simply to uplift but found you like to lie elsewhere.

But you will always need me and my love for you will never cease we remain one even in death.

And before you speak I forgive you as I know you are closer to me than I am to myself.

Earthly Minds

Before I return to the dust which formed an animate vessel in the image and likeness in which the giver of life intended, enclosing within the essence of the endless heavens, the fragile nature of which kept me close to an unknown threshold.

I pray that ages pass while I face this path and as the seasons change the rains and wind go back from whence they came, as the appearance of the surface is altered from warm and pleasant to cold and creviced, all light grows dim but not so far as my eyes see clearly.

The closer I saw my goal approach the more rapidly the strength of my steps grew weary, I wish that those that passed could relay to me a message, but the only news that came was that those that left would never again be within my physical presence.

They are as dear to my heart as my breath to its body, their blood still flows like the air through my mouth and nostrils, so I exhale in the trail of life and although both are unseen I still sense the spirit within both them and me.

Although the breath they possessed was long ago silenced, I still hear their footsteps and witness their image in my mind's eye as they whisper to my conscience, and like a child's first steps by soothing words I'm helped along, apprehension transferred into fixed intentions changed into longing to embrace a new form.

Physicals concern for Sol

The first rays of the sun are the most uplifting and thankfully in my day of need you came to me just as swiftly, I transcend my problems like the sun ascends the morning but when will they end now that a new day is dawning. Erstwhile the dawn brought a brighter smile but now with the light of life slowly subsiding it has become hard to retreat from the quiet embrace of sleep. So you stay near me when I need company and if you should make any judgments about my inconsistencies then I plead, do it for the love of me, our companionship is alike the heart and mind, one will perish without the other and no progress can be made without compromise. Thus we step firmly although slowly, advancing one day at a time, constantly maintaining a straight line while seeking a pure life that we may be holy, because you taught me we can never maintain life giving lessons without direction, so where you go I will follow with undying patience and renewed affection.

When alone amongst the multitude I found their way to be the path of the aimless, and I see it's best to maintain your solitude and be rejected when you are asked to sell your very essence for acceptance. A grave accepts all who are lowered into it just as does the empty hole in the heart of those who lead a soulless existence, they are superior to me like tomorrow is to yesterday, but we both will reach the same goal when my breath is exhausted they will be present, we both will be absorbed by the same soil. Could I assume credit for something I had no part in making and would I be justified in imposing my will upon sovereign nations, like this do they pass judgments those who had no place in creation, and those who make false statements lose all trust, for them I have put all sympathy aside and I pray for their desolation because from below and above they have lost all love.

Thus do I always hold onto my beloved we were separated after my adolescents but once again I found your essence, to determine our origin is like finding the starting point of free flowing wind, so on the back of a soft breeze should you call me, the sun and its warmth cannot be separated and one instant without you is sincerely missed, so be my light I will raise you up that we may meet our zenith in this existence, and thereby shine upon what we seek, before you instructed me I kept my grief concealed between my tongue and cheek, now I press my pen my soul left manifest through ink.

Regal in my pain

Didn't I transcend my burden much like the livestock ascends the herdsman, why would I prefer to be stingy with the thing that fed me lavishly, salivated at my fattening and now has cause to sacrifice me?

In truth I tasted of this illusion, and it never fulfilled me, on the contrary it took from me plenty and on the inside reduced my excess to empty.

I considered as life's source poured through closed eyes and consequently the world around me became demystified.

I was questioned about my domestication, further pain came with my reply, the vain cannot feel my hunger pains and the deaf cannot hear my cries, in truth was my response, although a lie would have alleviated the pain that it brought.

Empathy for my body

If only I could see ahead so I know I would be there to stare back, with memories scattered as in the wind I once again recall my tracks, in a moment of realization I reclaimed immaterial property, retracing from adulthood to the mind state of a child when I was the recipient of pleasant feelings and lively smiles, back then this was my transient reality.

I looked forward innocently with sincere intent to imprint my essence upon impermanent things, but matter was slow to allow itself to be molded into the image of my dreams, without senses there was no limitations to the scenery and everything in existence only displayed the characteristics they were faced with, I projected myself and reflected your spirit, but with time nonexistent I failed to bring events into proper sequence.

My temporal companion you abandoned my presence, so now I longed for the love and compassion which is only to be found in the heavens, I was stranded in barren landscapes and wished to be returned to the familiar embrace of the womb from which I was birthed, but I can only pray that one day we will be found far away from this world and once again close to the earth.

Set in stone

From immemorial before the currents of time surfaced when the earth with its own hand carved inscriptions revealing unto the heavens what was inwardly hidden, motion emerged with a stone's throw traversing the landscapes with swiftness by its own volition, as the wind whispers its familiar message in the expanse of the directions, the flow of life has changed but always will it maintain its essence.

I stand in place although I'm everywhere life is known, I presented my image to life and freely gave away my properties internally unto animate things, the structure of the bones and teeth that I assist with life's maintenance and the absorption of sustenance, so it may be reanimated and returned to me providing the foundation for the germ of fertility, now I witness the plants and trees and all things come into fruition.

For multitudes untold I provide a loving home, and when I decay it's not that I have passed away I simply relinquished my place that life may manifest in a new form, this is my gift as I'm not bound to the ground, I may descend to you from the sky I make a trail through the heavens the radiance of my tail in the likeness of starlight keeping me in flight like feathers, so reflect upon longevity when you witness me, as my life commenced from the beginning and I will continue to be beyond the end of this existence.

Empathy for my spirit

*I can only roam so far before I'm faced with a barrier, so now I pray in
retrospect of past mistakes that future moves will fare better.*

*Through any obstacles we would walk hand in hand but now facing the
current in isolation I stand.*

*Your companionship was unstable to me it fell apart through lack of
maintenance and after parting ways I can only speculate as to if we
share the same frustrations.*

*A bird cannot separate from its wings that's why I would rather you
ascend to the heavens with me, than be bound to the ground and
plagued with inconsistencies.*

*When I lie down to sleep you leave me with longing, while I'm alone
you roam and experience things of which I can only dream.*

*And when you return from your absence and become questioned with
aspects of which you cannot answer, you begin to speak to me of images
and scenes I could scarcely believe.*

*But beyond anything I trust in you and I trust it's true that when you
leave temporarily you will place a prayer in the air for me.*

Never will I miss the soulless

Before you came I did not know hell existed, it first became a concern with the unveiling of your appearance.

So you condemned me to suffering just by your presence, but from adherence to love and a childlike innocence it appeared to me at first that your company was ordained by the very heavens.

Through an affectionate union we exchanged sacraments but as time would tell you held nothing sacred.

You came arrayed in white under the guise of matrimony but I looked behind the reflection of colorless eyes and saw that you see nothing holy.

My father does not know you and you have become my mother's enemy, I know that death will do us part but in my heart you are already a memory.

They too shall pass

As a prisoner to your imposition upon me I'm turned away from the love of life and being blinded by your lies I see, only the love of truth shall set me free, because gradually you procure everything and if I found it within myself to forgive and forget and pick up whatever you had left, I would surely turn to you the other cheek but you would only return to me the kiss of death.

I have acquired your selfish ways by being exposed to your energy and so I see that a people became a reflection of the company to which they cling, and the most apparent characteristic they acquired from your company was that a forked tongue can justify anything.

Traversing land and water just to alter the likeness of creation into the image of disease, may the providence above resurrect our lives and renew our love, those worthy of blame may seek shade but they will only evaporate within the light of a new day.

Because if left alone they would corrupt even the sky and then expand into the heavens, and because of this it became obvious that their transgression went beyond all penitence, artificial things have shown themselves as shallow on the surface decaying on the inside and soon to disappear from earthly existence.

Solitary mirage

The fear I felt was no less than uncertainty, in the time I thought would be wasted I tasted this urgency.

I seen before me an ideal path to heal, because past injuries had dulled my senses and lessened my proficiency.

I called for help but no one heard me, but in the matter of health it was more than enough that I heard myself.

I grew weak from the smell of blood but worse it was to see myself suffer in the reflection of self–love.

Because I seek myself like fear seeks security, but certainly when fear subsides the comfort of the heart overcomes the caution of the mind.

Embraced in every direction

Raise me like the warmth raising gentle blades, I'm cooled by the embrace of the all-encompassing night and caressed in the morning by your tender rays.

I ascend in the essence of time after I'm sustained by condensation; sustenance comes to me on the back of a gentle breeze.

In the light I stand erect continually, but from a passionate tempest I'm laid flat if only momentarily.

I absorbed my provision with little effort, but in life I find that things change and my fortune comes and goes with the weather.

But what I rely on in life is mine by birth, and as I continue to exist may it never leave my presence.

My peace comes from below providing growth and the comfort of acceptance, and from above I progress my love descends from the heavens.

Newly born

From the first time I opened my eyes I witnessed the truth eager to see the earth the heavens and all things until the world obscured my view, I could not claim as mine those that lead lives devoid of spirit it is sacrilege to pass judgment on others characteristics and appearance, as the traits they are given they could not help as they did not create themselves, and in the same way they and I had no control over our earthly lives and between the extremes of sickness and health were powerless to anticipate our moment of death.

If they disapprove of my way of life and seek to artificially alter my mode all they will meet with will be frustration and loss of imagined control, and when I will not fit into their definition it is right to label me as an animal, because surely the progeny of the earth know the maker of the universe formed them first, we share space with those similar in form but opposite in composition.

If the maker made us of the same mold they would cling to my company, because like luminous stars which gradually fade with the sun's appearance countless have came and went before our existence, days have appeared and passed and the fact that we share the same space and time in our short span of life must have some significance, good feeling between offspring brings smiles to the parents but dissension in the household brings cause for its foundation to crumble.

Tree of life

*May I pick you from your solitude although in truth it was you who found me,
I stand in awe of your interest as you stand out from your surroundings.*

*I graciously consume your company like fruit for the hungry and although
you are within arm's length, in sincerity I would climb all limbs to remove you
from the loftiest tree.*

*And by this gain the fulfillment of knowledge and understanding, through the
consumption of your love for me I would gladly extend my patience and surely
endure suffering.*

*And by my digestion comes cessation of isolation, as sweet things pass
through my system nourishing my appetite for company.*

*I will return the excess to fertile ground with likeness to soil which resurrects
may it blend in undistinguished, with energy reborn may it provide growth
and renewed existence to a new form.*

*Out of love all life is seeded so let our hearts be planted firmly in our
intentions, with every beat intend to grow with me that we may witness our
love grow into fruition.*

Favorite Son

Awoke as one from a dream yet I'm wakeful continually, in anticipation of the revival of my mind's eye, I focus the rays of deep thought upon what has already transpired.

Tranquil I come emergent from a path immersed in darkness, to be raised in radiance my first day, beheld while bathed in scarlet.

Hereafter I only emerged to bring my love to the earth, through birth I'm brought forward, heaven sent to appear and reveal the light behind all existence.

Everywhere I'm the light of my household, so may my family revel in the warmth of my company, may my life run its course in goodness, and my essence travel through the blood of my descendants, but I will travel alone since only relatives are allowed within my midst.

Revive as I arrive, although silent I conveyed my message with ease, so please heed my words as I call for abundance, and follow my first footsteps as I walk above all else.

Risen, against the wind

It is true that every beginning has an end, I recollect in between as I press my pen.

Reanimating scenes in which moments fly away on the wings of eternity.

And like a dream I failed to bring everything into its proper place.

The once timeless imprints upon my vision have entered my mind and became condensed into an instant.

So near to what I lived but so distant from what I envisioned.

I held aloft my thoughts to ascend the tempestuous winds of a clouded mind.

Thankfully harsh weather dissipated paving the way for life giving light.

Now my heart is light like a feather may it once again take flight.

Hence in the present time I 'am no longer grounded in my previous existence.

I turn the page paving the way to read my future and became uplifted.

Outside of me you have nothing

Whatever comes to be quickly becomes a memory, in an instant you found love for me, yet now we part, since in a moment you became my enemy.

I wonder how childish ways can be contained in fully developed brains, and I see now that what transpires in time cannot be changed, so if I long for a companion I cling to my heart.

It compelled me to look at things with indifference, and counseled me to maintain a vast distance from the envious.

And who would be envious of me when whatever I had I gave away freely, therefore I starve for lack of sustenance.

And as I cannot live on bread alone I seek to supplement my needs with love and peace, but yet I'm continually thirsty for companionship.

Ironically what I need most slips thru my grasp like liquid, but from my experience I sense most are malnourished, so although I'm right I ask myself for forgiveness.

My masterpiece in pieces

Remember the moments when I used to hold you, by the passions of my actions my beloved, I did mold you.

You were barren soil made desolate through the arid condition of your past experiences, but like a wind I arrived in your life with swiftness, in your path I took a sure foothold and with my hands I made you malleable.

I carved a lively smile on a stone face, but a statue cannot respond to the pleas of a human being, I regret in retrospect that I attempted to sculpt you only for my own sake.

When I want something I realized I seek to restrict it to my solitary possession, deceiving myself into believing she's confined solely to my own love and affection.

I thought I was the focal part of her mind and heart, but now I see that before me others have occupied her feelings and consumed her thoughts, and now I'm grievous to know others were near as I was to my beloved, work of art.

Heavenly Bodies

The soothing shade gave way to a heated battle, because in the light of day there is left no place for the unnatural.

The right of life has been usurped upon the surface of the once pristine earth, but yet the right of life is also that rebirth must always follow death.

So may the truth and grace of past days once again resurrect.

I've rejected my tears and cut loose my hearts attachment, but it has returned like rain after drought and heavy famine.

I seek refuge from its violent downpour; the shower has caused me to tread a lonely road in order to find shelter.

My soles became worn and as my empathy increased I began to feel weak for those as yet to be born.

The way I went was rich in obstacles but the path of those who already passed became my present model.

In heavy rain I focused on the discomfort and failed to consider the future growth, I find that in all things you find aspects of both good and bad.

Thus hope can be acquired through any circumstance so I take fresh faith as I face a decaying path.

Even if I never see you again

The obstacles you faced I fully intended to chase away so when you reflect upon me envision a smile upon my face, as the fulfillment you see is simply a byproduct of the promises I make.

Do not fall in love with me as those that fall experience pain while those that see feel sorry, rather let us grow into an upright bond that we may become one heart with keen mind, divided between two bodies.

May my feelings be your property so we can accumulate the wealth of attachment and then I can feel content with what I possess, because I became reassured when I asked myself, who can squander love and affection?

I do prefer love to material property because as I reflected on reality I realized that wherever I will ultimately arrive, physical impediments would meet with their demise.

Whatever I make will slowly decay and its temporal importance will quickly subside, but with love I feel weightless in spirit, un-constricted at heart, and uplifted in mind, and I pray it may accompany me when I begin my journey over the great divide.

After time flies

What lies between the extremes of rejection and welcoming, in my ignorance I put forth a plea and pray it may be a relief to me.

Because even the things that shine the brightest become rusted when abandoned, as I opened my eyes and I'm no longer blind I find what I see is not what I imagined.

Because when I attempted to flee from what caught my eye, my hope became a fugitive, I couldn't stand to be imprisoned by a soulless existence and through the payment of my attention my senses grew weary.

Because material reality seemed so real and tangible in my mind but the veil became lifted the instant I closed my eyes, everything imaginable had its origin in my minds vision.

And with the recovery of my sight the reflection of my soul will begin to shine, and what cannot be touched cannot be confined, thus my essence slips through the grasp of the present hands of time.

Veiled becomes unveiled

Everybody possesses a body, and if you have only to give a part of it, you only can give what was loaned to you.

How vain it is for a body to exalt its flesh upon what it temporarily possess, when there is one above that owns all things.

Whoever has deemed the life of another as below theirs, how can this be true? When the lowest part of the Earth is in the ground and all life reaches that place.

All life, which are the expressions of the Earths face return to the ground and all possessions part ways in death.

Anyone among the living can end life but who amongst us can resurrect? The only thing I found irreplaceable was my soul, I know that whatever comes will come, but whatever comes must also go.

Expelled from my eyes

I sharpened pointless thoughts which pierced the back of my mind and the tears that sprung through flowed forth becoming droplets in the infinite currents of time, the pleasures of my heart have came and went, my disappointments have ascended my hopes so after retreating into the recesses of my chest I now begin my descent.

I wash away the traces of suffering which evaporate as I wept and of all the emotions in life that flow freely the worst to accept would have to be regret, to harbor longing for past seasons impedes present growth so it's best to seek comfort when seeing all of life's scenes between the cold of sorrow and the warmth of fresh hope, and the fact that in reality all these things will come and go in their various degrees.

And although different in their appearance it becomes apparent that the seasons do not appear but in sequence, after the fall of rain may the springs that flow from life's cold bring blessings, may my life be lengthened as I witness changes expressed through the length of my years, as I learn the lesson of seasons expressed through the embodiment of my tears.

Night loves day

I know my body is a vessel between which the spirit moves with fluidity, it pours forth from my heart to be consumed by the heavens a taste of nourishment for my memory.

My companion only open your mouth to me with compassion and you may satiate your thirst with my legacy.

May my excess meet your absence and through connection obtain balance, and by mutual exchange behold what is made, because many who fall short bring another into their place disgraced much the same.

The path of lonesomeness it does not lead to abundance in the life of living beings, and the proper course is to benefit my and your existence and to discard broken things.

If you are bound by honor don't attempt to escape from lack of trust in the face of hardship, what is considered of value must be kept safe and hidden away, than at the risk of theft being openly displayed.

So like the moon I become fully visible from your reflection and without your presence I lack half of myself in the likeness of a crescent, and through our union I fulfill the will of the heavens.

My Gift to the Present Sent From Heaven

I pray for synthesis in this existence and since I see the one above in our companionship my love is pure worship, through love all life was created and through its fulfillment we get an insight into the mind of its maker, and being divinely inspired it cannot subside even unto the afterlife and even with this being true, in consideration of all ones earthly accumulations it must be evident that you cannot take it with you, even so, it will always remain with my soul all of this life's experiences, so in the sequence of what I've seen and heard I'm in debt to your words.

From the former expressions of timeless eloquence I present a gift to my laureate, but from knowing I will leave these experiences and all those who shared with me in them I realize my life is an illusion of closeness. So through the cessation of time I wave good bye to its confines as well as to whatever they entail, If I could foretell my end and foresee my commencement I would bid farewell to the future, yet in retrospect what is the loss of ones company to me? In the seasonal changes of life it is nothing more than the loss of a leaf to a tree; therefore a temporal companion becomes a tempestuous blessing.

If only I could see through the many eyes that have came and went in this life, from the womb all have entered, upon the Earth they've expressed themselves and from whence they arrived now they have left, we awake by the Sun's rays and after the light of day slowly subsides the cycle of growth is set as we age and obtain rest in the night, we become covered in dust and return to the womb of an honored mother and between these extremes the soul seeks the body because in the course of life what is one without the other?

33

Before I was, there was existence and since my life is transient it is measured by thoughts of the transition, so now through humility I have contempt for pride and with sincerity I take heed to my hearts plea to mind, and within my heart and mind lies heavenly concepts and by words I have tried to convey that they have a presence in all of life's various aspects, but the truth of the reality of things both lofty and sublime are the most difficult to present before the gravity of earthly minds.

I came forth from lying down and was told I will one day lie down just as I had awoke, so in my wakefulness I' am thankful, and revived and remade that the worries of my heart may rest in the emergence of a renewed day, upon this hope depends all of Earths future growth, reflected in my breath as physicals concern for soul, as the Sun appears from within it radiates what the surface holds dear in the rays of vitality, so behold in all life we may see the living design of reciprocity, even though, now I witness the pristine surface being converted into waste, and through the misery that this conveys I'm still regal in my pain.

The mother who nurtures experienced many changes as her children were domesticated and the gifts she freely gave them have been forcibly taken, and ironically, they became prisoners of war even in peace, but be replenished my family the adversaries stratagem was intent to confine our physical but our souls will forever roam just as they were designed, without the constructs of time and free of needs, but in life's cycles I attain comfort as I know all things dead become rotted as if it never existed within memory forgotten.

From the Earth and the essence of life that gave birth to its existence through the spirit breathed into me I revive empathy for my body, since the beginning of earthly existence from the formation of vegetation and its continual growth, all things pass through the realm of the unseen and as such all things are foretold, thus those who sculpted the pristine Earth into their image, their decay and eventual disappearance are eternally set in stone.

By the breath I breathe I need most that which to this life is intrinsic, so with the gift that is existence I receive empathy for my spirit, may it be as inseparable to me as life is to everything, indeed they are one and the same therefore my aim is to simply be complete. One cannot be whole less it be known from whence they came my forefathers sparkle above and my mother lie's dignified below, and in between these all living beings come and go. Others have usurped my birthright and seek to render me hopeless, so in the birth of a new day when we forever part ways never will I miss the soulless.

A guilty face is uncovered and is no longer hidden by an innocent mask, and after all the falsehood spoken had covered the truth, as time would tell they too shall pass. From the landscapes is erased their abodes and the manifestation of their actions, a transparent existence fades away as if it was a solitary mirage undistinguished from something imagined, as the void and darkness is replenished may Earths children be embraced in every direction like blades of grass and as they sprout forth in delicate and tender forms, life becomes as its mother, from the womb rebirthed newly born.

*In manifesting the essence of life from the fertile growth of the Earths
seed as the tree of life providing growth and acceptance to all things,
and as I ascend in the warmth of the rays of vitality uncovered in the
light of day and raised by love, I'm brought to maturity being guided by
the maker of life's favorite son, and from the maker I'm given a lofty gift
my spirit risen, against the wind and being exposed to relief may it
provide my soul with peace, the prospect of security to my body and as
all things exist within my perception they speak "outside of me you have
nothing".*

*From the fruition of the knowledge of good and evil when a forked
tongue beguiled the Earths progeny, although blinded by deceit
I still see my masterpiece in pieces, and as of now I grieve, although we
will surely witness the Earths children be reborn in Heavenly bodies, so
may my relations in life adhere to patience and keep close at heart the
fact that there is a beginning to every ending, in the end even if I never
see you again my remembrance gives credence to my existence, so may
it stay stationary within your mind after time flies that you may become
uplifted.*

*As darkness is the forebear of light and by the force of its will what was
veiled becomes unveiled, now my tears are still as I regain my sight and
the reflection of my soul will begin to shine as living water is expelled
from my eyes, night loves day and by their union the birth of the
morning came, synthesis is heaven sent, and as the time nears I bring to
light my gift to the present.*